GENERAL KNOWLEDGE BOOKKEEPING & ACCOUNTS

Moses Carson B   **ACCA (Aff) BA/EDUC, DBA**

© **Copy right**
All rights reserved. No part of this publication may be reproduced, stored in a retrieval system, or transmitted in any form, or by any means, electronic, mechanical, photocopying, recording, or otherwise without the written permission of the copyright owner.

FIRST EDITION   **JANUARY 2008**

Other books by the same author;
- Bookkeeping & Accounts Simplified
- Bookkeeping & Accounts for Beginners
- Basic Commerce
- Accounting for BGCSE
- Accounts for High School
- Accounts for O Level
- Bookkeeping & Accounts Revision
- Bookkeeping & Accounts Questions & Answers
- IGCSE Accounting

D1528400

Published by Custom Books, UK Ltd

Email: custom.books@yahoo.co.uk
Website: www.custombooks.org

ISBN 978-1-906380-09-0

PREFACE

This book is written by an ACCA Qualified Accountant, a professional teacher, and an experienced writer with many titles.

Its designed for the general reader, who is interested in knowing how bookkeeping and Accounts is done.

It gives the reader an opportunity to understand what goes on between the recording of documents, and the outcome in form of Accounts.

The jargon, terminologies, and procedures are all explained.

So far, its the only book which explains the straight forward accounting practice, without using the unfriendly debit and credit.

It provides background information for those interested in the bookkeeping and accounting profession.

Its layout and illustrations provide a very relaxing and interesting read.

Its well written, reader friendly, and very easy to understand.

ACKNOWLEDGEMENT

Special thanks to my wife Immaculate, and our children for all their support while compiling this book.

CONTENTS

Chapter 1

INTRODUCTION

Bookkeeping is the classification, recording and verification of business transactions. Its done by a **Bookkeeper** on a monthly, quarterly, or annual basis.

To **classify** is to separate receipt and payment documents since they are recorded separately. We also identify the columns in which each document is to be recorded.

To **verify** is to confirm that what was recorded is correct. Control accounts are prepared and the balances confirmed with a separate set of records like a bank statement.

A business is an activity set up with the aim of generating income and profit for its owners.

Activities which generate income involve some form of **payment**, and a **receipt** of money from a sale or a charge for services. These activities are known as **transactions**.

Accounting is the verification of annual bookkeeping records, preparation of final accounts, and the interpretation of results. This is done by an **Accountant**. However, an Accountant can do both Bookkeeping and Accounting.

Accounts are prepared following a set of procedures and accounting rules.

Final accounts are summarised statements which show the profit or loss, and what the business owns and owes. They include a profit and loss account, and balance sheet.

A profit and loss account is a statement prepared to show the profit or loss made by a business.

A balance sheet is a statement which shows what a business owns and what it owes. Before anybody buys a business, they need to know what it owns and owes.

In addition to the above functions, Accounts are prepared because its required by **law**. The accounts show a profit which is a basis of determining how much **tax** to pay. Bank managers and other investors may be interested in accounting information.

The procedures explained in this book focus on the transactions of a small sole trader, who buys and sells on a cash basis only. There is no credit. Partnerships and limited Companies issues are mentioned briefly towards the end.

A credit transaction is where the buyer is allowed to pay after 30 to 90 days. The buyer becomes a **debtor** and the seller becomes a **creditor**.

Although some payments are made by credit card, they are treated as cash transactions. The reason is, the buyer authorises the immediate transfer of payment to the seller's account.

Payment by cheque is a cash transaction. Although the transfer or clearing of a cheque takes up to 5 working days, its not a credit transaction.

A profit is the amount left after deducting expenses from income.

A loss is when the expenses are bigger than income generated. This means the income was not large enough to pay for expenses. So the extra expenses are paid for, using the invested capital. So a loss is the amount of capital lost in a business.

Capital is money or other items brought by owners into a business, with the aim of making profit.

Income is a receipt, but not all receipts are an income.

A receipt is any money received in a business and it includes; sales, takings, capital, loans, and others.

An income is money generated through business activity. An example is sales.

Sales is the value of what was sold. It may be referred to as **takings** or **turnover**.

Borrowed money and capital contributions are not income.

Expenses are a payment, but not all payments are an expense. This is explained in chapter 8.

Accounts are prepared for a **financial year**, which is a period of 12 months. Each business decides when its financial year starts. The end becomes automatic, after 12 months.

HISTORY OF BOOKKEEPING AND ACCOUNTING

Bookkeeping and accounting are very old procedures which date back to the early days of civilization in Mesopotamia, present day Iraq and Iran.

They needed to maintain accurate records for agricultural products and their values.

Simple Accounting is mentioned in the Christian New Testament Bible (Matt. 25:19), and the Islamic Quran (2:282).

The first book on Bookkeeping was written in 1458 by Benedetto, a merchant in modern day Croatia, although it wasn't published.

The first publication of the bookkeeping system used by Venetian Merchants was by an Italian, Luca Pacioli in 1496.

The first known book in the English language was published in London by John Gouge in 1543.

This was followed by a short book of instructions in 1588, by John Mellis of Southwark, England.

An other book was published by an Accountant, Richard Dafforne in 1635. He published a second edition in 1636, a third edition in 1656, and a fourth edition in 1684.

From then onwards, many Accountants and Teachers have written about bookkeeping and accounting.

Chapter 2

STAGES IN ACCOUNTS PREPARATION

There are two stages in the preparation of Accounts. We start with Bookkeeping and end with Accounting.

For the sake of simplicity, this book focuses on a business which buys and sells for cash only. Aspects of a credit business are towards the end.

Please note; for a cash business, the **ledger** is not required. So the **trial balance** is also not required.

However, there is some explanation in chapter 14 to 17.

Bookkeeping is to do with the recording of all money received and paid out.

All money received is recorded in a receipts analysis.

All payments are recorded in a payments analysis.

After all transactions are recorded and verified using periodic control accounts, bookkeeping ends and we start the accounting phase.

Accounting starts by generating annual summaries from the periodical bookkeeping records.

Next we prepare annual control accounts. Identify the adjustments to be made.

We then prepare the profit and loss account, and lastly the balance sheet.

Below is an illustration of the stages we go through;

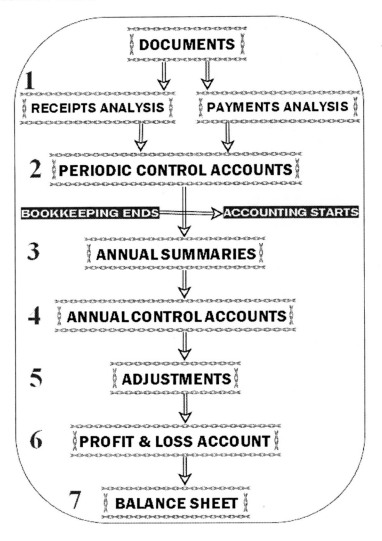

Chapter 3

THE RECEIPTS ANALYSIS

This chapter explains where money received is recorded. How its recorded, and confirmed to be error free.

A business receives money in cash and cheque form. If it accepts electronic payments then some is received by debit and credit cards.

All money received by the bank and recorded on the client's bank account is **banking**. This includes cash and cheque deposits, receipts by debit or credit cards, transfers, interest, loans, and others.

All cash and banking is recorded in a receipts analysis, and we have an illustration on the following page.

This analysis has two sections; the receipt methods, and the receipts classification.

Receipt method refers to how the money was received. In this case it was received by either cash or banking. Each of these is allocated a column just after the date.

Receipts classification refers to the different sources of money. Some of it comes from takings, deposits, interest, loans, and others.

Takings are sales made and the money is received in form of cash or cheques.

Some of the payments are received by debit or credit cards.

New Fashions

Receipts Analysis

April 2006

	Receipt Methods			Receipts Classification			
Date	Cash	Banking	Takings	Deposits	Interest	Loans
1-Apr-06	137.85	3,000.00	137.85			3,000.00
3-Apr-06	64.85	-	64.85			
4-Apr-06	150.35	-	150.35			
5-Apr-06	153.00	-	153.00			
6-Apr-06	187.67	-	187.67			
7-Apr-06	99.65	650.00	99.65	650.00		
8-Apr-06	168.40	-	168.40			
10-Apr-06	86.25	-	86.25			
11-Apr-06	174.25	-	174.25			
12-Apr-06	129.75	-	129.75			
13-Apr-06	158.45	-	158.45			
14-Apr-06	158.50	-	158.50			
15-Apr-06	60.50	-	60.50			
17-Apr-06	91.00	-	91.00			
18-Apr-06	118.00	-	118.00			
19-Apr-06	145.50	-	145.50			
20-Apr-06	112.48	-	112.48			
21-Apr-06	147.50	950.00	147.50	950.00		
22-Apr-06	73.65	-	73.65			
24-Apr-06	84.35	-	84.35			
25-Apr-06	124.00	-	124.00			
26-Apr-06	154.75	-	154.75			
27-Apr-06	137.82	-	137.82			
28-Apr-06	124.45	-	124.45			
29-Apr-06	114.20	11.07	114.20		11.07	
	3,157.17	4,611.07	3,157.17	1,600.00	11.07	3,000.00

Receipt Methods   7,768.24
Receipts Classification   7,768.24

All takings are recorded in the cash column, even if some were received by cheque or card. The aim is to have all sales monitored on one account, the cash account.

The exception to this are credit sales explained in chapter 16. Larger businesses may record takings separately from cash.

Takings are initially recorded per transaction. As soon as a sale is made, a record is put down. It may be in form of a receipt, a till slip, an invoice, or in a sales record book.

Individual transactions are added up to get the total for the day. Other businesses get the day's total by counting cash at the end of the day, and deducting the cash which was available at the start of day.

Its the daily total which we record in the receipts analysis.

Takings are recorded twice. Once in the receipts method, in this case its the cash column. The second recording is made in the takings column, which is among the receipt's classification.

An example is the takings on the 1st of April totaling £137.85. We start by recording the date, followed by the amount in the takings column. We finish by recording the same £137.85 in the cash column. This is illustrated on the previous page.

Total takings are recorded for all the days of the month,

and for all months of the year.

In the banking column is recorded all monies received by the bank on behalf of the business. We extract this information from bank statements.

In our illustration we have classification columns for deposits, interest, and loans.

In the deposits column we record cash and cheques deposited with the bank. For example, on the 7th of April, there was a deposit of £650.

We start with the date, and record the amount in the deposits column among the classifications. If there is another type of banking on that day, we add them together. Its their total that we record in the banking column in the receipt methods. In this case its only the £650.

In the interest column is recorded interest received from the bank. In the loans column we record any loans received.

For businesses which receive payments by debit or credit card, the amounts are recorded in the cards analysis column. Money introduced by the owner is recorded in the capital column.

At month end we get totals for each column. Before this analysis is completed, we **confirm if the records and additions are correct.**

This is done by ensuring the total for **receipt methods** is the same as the total for the **receipts classification**.

In our illustration we add cash to banking and get £7,768.24.

We also add totals for all the receipts classification and get £7,768.24.

Since the two totals are the same, we confirm the records are correct.

A difference in the totals implies there is at least one **error**. This is investigated and corrected before continuing.

This receipts analysis is recorded monthly or quarterly, depending on how often the client brings in the records.

The cash and banking totals are used on the monthly or quarterly control accounts as explained in chapter 5.

The receipts classification totals are used to prepare annual summaries.

Recording the receipts analysis is generally not difficult. Picking up the date is the easiest. If the takings records from the supplier are detailed, we summarise to get daily totals.

All the banking information is picked up from the bank statement. The only tricky part is identifying the column in which to classify, or record it.

The day's record is finalised by getting the cash and bank totals. The same procedure is followed for all the days of the month, and all months in the year.

There is no details column in this receipts analysis. What we could record in it doesn't differ much. So we rely on the various column titles. Its only in rare circumstances, when the source of receipt needs to be individually specified.

DISHONOURED CHEQUES

These are cheques where the bank refuses to make payment. They are also referred to as **bounced cheques**.

They are identified on the bank statement when the same figure appears in both the **paid out and paid in columns.** The dates on which they are recorded are not very far apart.

The second entry is made to reverse the first one. So it ends up with no effect on the bank balance.

There is neither a receipt nor a payment. You can't say it paid for anything. Nor can you say you received any money.

Since the banking and payments analysis are prepared after receiving the bank statement, dishonoured cheques **are not recorded**

So each of the two identical figures is just marked on the bank statement with a cancelled C ('C') and that's it.

This means that each figure marked with a cancelled 'C' is cancelled by an equivalent figure in the opposite column on the bank statement.

Whether the dishonoured cheque was received or paid out, the treatment is the same.

Chapter 4

THE PAYMENTS ANALYSIS

This chapter explains what is recorded in the payments analysis. How its recorded, and confirmed to be error free.

Payments made by a business are recorded in a payments analysis.

The source of information are receipts, invoices, and bank statements.

Receipts and invoices are organised neatly and filed.

Each document is given an internally generated identification number before recording. If the starting number is 1, then it helps to know how many documents they are.

This number eases the process of searching for information when we have to refer to the document itself.

From the filed documents, a payments analysis is prepared, as illustrated on the following page.

Payments are recorded individually from each document, and not added to get daily totals, like its done for receipts.

Analysis books are bought with the columns already drawn. The date, details, reference number, and total columns are obvious. Discretion is only required when deciding which payment is recorded in which analysis column.

General Knowledge Bookkeeping & Accounts

New Fashions   **Payment Analysis**   **April 2006**

Ref	Date	Details	Payment Methods			Purchases	Payment Analysis													
			Cash	Bank	Credit card		Direct Expenses	Salaries & Wages	Premises Costs	Repairs & Maintenance	Gen Admin	Motor Expenses	Legal & Profes sional	Bank & finance charges	Interest Charges	Sundry Expenses	FA above £100	Drawings	Credit card repaymt	Loan repaymt
	01-Apr-06	Bookshop			15.75						15.75									
	04-Apr-06	Sam-Drawings	140.00															140.00		
	05-Apr-06	I & J-Stock		478.09		478.09														
	07-Apr-06	Packaging			18.40											18.40				
	08-Apr-06	Nico-Personal		8.80														8.80		
	11-Apr-06	Sam-Drawings	140.00															140.00		
	12-Apr-06	Fashions -Stock		811.61		811.61														
	12-Apr-06	Dex-Stock			207.50	207.50														
	12-Apr-06	G Textiles-Stock		332.92		332.92														
	13-Apr-06	Sam-Drawings	140.00															140.00		
	20-Apr-06	G Textiles-Stock		301.83		301.83														
	24-Apr-06	B & Q-Stool			15.00		15.00													
	25-Apr-06	Sam-Drawings	140.00															140.00		
	25-Apr-06	Raves-Stock		371.38		371.38														
	25-Apr-06	Rent	260.00						260.00											
	27-Apr-06	Card repayment		256.65															256.65	
	28-Apr-06	Wages	346.66					346.66												
	28-Apr-06	Loan & Interest		137.50											12.50					125.00
	30-Apr-06	Bank chgs		11.95										11.95						
		Payment methods	1,166.66	2,170.73	256.65	2,503.33	15.00	346.66	260.00	-	15.75	-	-	11.95	12.50	18.40	-	568.80	256.65	125.00
		Total Payments	4,134.04																	
			4,134.04																	

Since this illustration is small and not clear, we divide it into two and lay one section below the other,

on the following page.

New Fashions — Payment Analysis — April 2006

			Payment Methods			Payment Analysis Columns		
Ref	Date	Details	Cash	Bank	Credit card	Purchases	Direct Expenses	Salaries & Wages
	01-Apr-06	Bookshop			15.75			
	04-Apr-06	Sam-Drawings	140.00					
	05-Apr-06	I & J -Stock		478.09		478.09		
	07-Apr-06	Packaging			18.40			
	08-Apr-06	Nico-Personal		8.80				
	11-Apr-06	Sam-Drawings	140.00					
	12-Apr-06	Fashions -Stock		811.61		811.61		
	12-Apr-06	Dex-Stock			207.50	207.50		
	12-Apr-06	G Textiles-Stock		332.92		332.92		
	18-Apr-06	Sam-Drawings	140.00					
	20-Apr-06	G Textiles-Stock		301.83		301.83		
	24-Apr-06	B & Q-Stool			15.00		15.00	
	25-Apr-06	Sam-Drawings	140.00					
	25-Apr-06	Raves-Stock		371.38		371.38		
	25-Apr-06	Rent	260.00					
	27-Apr-06	Card repayment		256.65				
	28-Apr-06	Wages	346.66					346.66
	28-Apr-06	Loan & Interest		137.50				
	30-Apr-06	Bank chgs		11.95				
			1,166.66	2,710.73	256.65	2,503.33	15.00	346.66
	Payment methods		4,134.04					
	Total Payments		4,134.04					

Payment Analysis Columns

Premises Costs	Repairs & Maintenance	Gen Admin	Motor Expenses	Legal & Professional	Bank & finance charges	Interest Charges	Sundry Expenses	FA above £100	Drawings	Credit card repaymt	Loan repaymt
		15.75									
									140.00		
							18.40				
									8.80		
									140.00		
									140.00		
									140.00		
260.00											
										256.65	
						12.50					125.00
					11.95						
260.00	-	15.75	-	-	11.95	12.50	18.40	-	568.80	256.65	125.00

The date, details, reference number, and total are copied from the receipt or invoice.

In the details column is written the supplier's name or what was paid for. This information is helpful when questions are asked. It could be a tax inspector asking two years later.

The columns for recording payments are classified into two. The payment methods and the payment analysis.

The three common **payment methods** are; cash, bank, and credit card. Each one is allocated a column and that is where the first entry or recording is made.

The first entry is made in the cash column if it was paid by cash. In the bank column if it was paid by cheque or debit card. And recorded in the credit card column if it was paid by credit card.

The second recording is made in one of the **payment analysis columns**.

There are occasions when one payment has two entries in the payment analysis columns.

For example, a single cheque used to pay for books for resale, and a ream of paper for use in the business. The books cost is recorded in the purchases column, while the ream's cost is recorded in the general administration column. That is where stationary is recorded.

When we add the two separated second entries, they should add up to the single entry in the bank column. At times it's a credit card paying for more than one type of payment.

This allocation of columns helps to isolate the business and non business payments. The business payments are classified according to a generally accepted format, among accounting and tax authorities.

A 24 column analysis book is sufficient for a small cash business. A bigger and more complex business may need more columns.

Once the receipts and invoices have been filed, the process of recording the reference or document number, date, supplier, and the amount in the payment method is not that difficult.

A document whose amount appears on the bank statement is recorded in the bank column.

A document whose amount appears on the credit card statement is recorded in the credit card column.

All the other documents whose amounts don't appear on either of the two statements, are recorded in the cash column.

The tricky part may be identifying the analysis column in which to make the second entry. What some suppliers provide is not obvious. Although we use experience, we at times consult the client to get accurate information.

After recording all figures in the payment method and the payment analysis columns, the next step is confirming if the whole analysis was done correctly.

The figures in each column are added up, and totals recorded at the bottom of each. The cash, bank and credit card column totals are added to get the total amount paid out. In this case it's a total of £4,134.04 for the month of April 2006.

We also add the totals for all payment analysis columns. The figure we get should be the same as the total amount paid. In our illustration the total is £4,134.04.

This is the **cross-casting** of the two sections separately. Its what we use to prove the records and additions are correct. Any difference means an error(s), which is investigated and corrected before continuing. This

procedure replaces the need to prepare a trial balance.

This is done monthly, quarterly, or annually depending on when the records are received.

The column totals are used to prepare the periodic and annual summaries and control accounts. The annual totals end up on the profit and loss account and balance sheet.

Below is a brief explanation for each of the payment types or analysis columns.

In the **Purchases column** we record goods bought for resale, or the raw materials bought for use in producing other goods for resale.

In the **Direct Expenses column** we record; the cost of hiring machines and equipment; small tools costing less than £100 that can't be recorded as fixed assets; and any other consumables bought. These expenses are incurred directly in regard to what was sold.

In the **Employee costs column** we record payments made towards salaries, wages, bonuses, and national insurance contributions.

In the **Premises costs column** we record payments made towards rent, business rates or council tax, bills for water, light, and heat. Plus any payments for property insurance and security.

In the **Repairs and Maintenance column** we record payments made towards the repair or maintenance of business premises, machinery, and equipment.

In the **General Administrative expenses** column we record payments for telephone and internet, postages, stationery, printing costs, and any other general office expenses.

In the **Motor Expenses** column we record payments made for petrol, diesel, repairs and servicing, insurance, road license, hire and leasing charges, parking charges, and AA/RAC membership.

In the **Travel and subsistence** column we record payments made for all travel costs including rail, air, taxis, trains, and buses. Hotel accommodation and subsistence on business trips are also recorded in this column.

Subsistence refers to food items bought because they are at work for the business.

In the **Advertising and promotions** column we record payments made for advertising, sales promotions, mail shots and the costs of entertaining clients.

In the **Legal and professional** column we record fees paid to Accountants, Solicitors, Surveyors, Architects, and any other professionals.

In the **Bad Debts** column we record money which debtors have failed to pay. This expense or loss of money is experienced by businesses selling on credit.

In the **Bank Charges** column we record charges by banks and credit card companies. In addition to monthly charges, there are loan and overdraft arrangement charges.

The finance Interest column is used for recording any kind of interest paid on borrowed money. This includes overdrafts and loans from banks, credit card companies, hire purchase, leasing and others. However, the repayment of borrowed money itself is recorded in either the credit card or loans column.

The **Sundry Expenses** column is for business expenses not recorded in any other column. They are rare expenses which are often small in amount.

In the **Fixed Assets** column we record payments for land and buildings, vehicles, plant and equipment, fixtures and fittings, and computer equipment.

This includes anything whose value is above £100, and is used in the business for more than one year.

Payments not made for business but personal issues are recorded in the **drawings column.**

Drawings is money or goods taken from the business for the owner's personal use.

However, they are only recorded if they were paid using money from the business. If they were paid using personal money, then they **are not** recorded among payments made by the business.

The **credit card repay** column is where we record money paid back to credit card companies. Any interest or other charges are recorded either in the bank charges or interest column.

Any loan repayments are recorded in the **loan repay column.** The charges and interest are recorded in the other columns as mentioned above.

PERIODIC CONTROL ACCOUNTS

This chapter explains how periodic receipts and payment analyses are checked against other records. This is done to confirm that balances in the bookkeeping records do agree with the cash available, and the bank statement balance.

After recording the receipts and payments analyses, control accounts are prepared.

The aim is to confirm if the bookkeeping balance does agree with another source of balance.

An example is bank. We have banking and payments recorded separately. Their correctness is individually confirmed.

However, there is need to confirm that what is recorded, agrees with the bank statement balance. On the following page is a bank control account for the first month of April 2006.

The value in and value out are used to simplify the debit and credit concepts. There is some deeper explanation in chapter 15 on the Ledger.

The control account is started with the opening balance at the start of the period. This should also be the opening balance on the bank statement. Total banking is extracted from the receipts analysis illustrated on page 8.

New Fashions

Bank Control Account

April 2006

	Value In	Value Out	
	Debits	Credits	Balance
Balance b/d			325.00
Banking	4,600.00		
Payments		2,710.73	
	4,600.00	2,710.73	**2,214.27**

Total payments are extracted from the bank payments total illustrated on page 14 and 15.

The last process is adding the opening balance to total receipts and deducting total payments. The answer is the balance which should be equal to the one on the bank statement.

There should be no difference since all information is extracted from the bank statement.

There is no need for a bank reconciliation if there is no difference between the control account and bank statement balance.

Please note that we are using vertical accounts and not the traditional "T" Accounts. Its easier to follow the value in and value out columns, than the debit and credit sides.

A control account is compiled for cash as illustrated below;

New Fashions			
Cash Control Account			
April 2006			
	Value In	Value Out	
	Debit	Credit	Balance
Balance b/d			124.00
Takings	3,157.17		
Deposits		1,600.00	
Paymts		1,166.66	
	3,157.17	2,766.66	**514.51**

This control account is for the first month of April 2006. It starts with the opening cash balance of £124. Total cash receipts are extracted from the receipts analysis illustrated on page 8. In this case all receipts came from takings.

Total deposits are extracted from the receipts analysis. Normally, this is extracted from the payments analysis. However, a deposits column was not added, to avoid congestion. What we get from the receipts analysis is the same figure and it serves the purpose.

Total payments are extracted from the cash payments total illustrated on page 14 and 15.

Total value in, is added to the opening balance. Total value out is deducted. What is left is the closing balance. This should be equal to the total notes and coins available in the business.

That is how this account helps to control the management of cash in the business.

If the available cash is less, we have to find out where it was spent. If its more, we have to find out where it came from.

The cash and bank control accounts are prepared whenever information is brought in and recorded.

If records are only brought in at the year end, then its done for all the 12 months, as we prepare the final accounts.

The cash and bank control accounts are prepared periodically since they are the most sensitive in the business.

However, the year end has more control accounts prepared, to cover the other aspects of the business.

THE ACCOUNTS FILE

This chapter explains the records generated in the process of preparing accounts, and how they are filed. There is an explanation of how they are related or cross referenced to each other.

After the year end, bookkeeping records are verified and the preparation of accounts starts.

Between the end of bookkeeping and the finalised accounts, much paper work is generated and they are known as **working papers.**

These papers are filed in what is called an **accounts file**. A file is opened for each client.

On this file you find information showing how each of the figures in the final accounts were derived.

The records follow a certain order that is indicated on an **index page.** This page is always on top of the working papers. It also serves as a checklist of what should be covered in the process.

As we prepare the working papers, we indicate where each of the figures is computed. So there is a filing reference besides each figure.

The aim is to guide whoever is looking through the accounts, to trace where each figure was derived. When they get to the reference page, they can see how it was computed.

However, the accounts for a sole trader and a partnership are not as comprehensive as those for a limited company.

Accounts for a cash business tend to be brief as compared to those for a credit business. So you may find some issues on the checklist not covered.

On the following page is an index page illustrated.

At the top is the client's name, file number, the year for which accounts are prepared for, and the staff who prepared them.

In **Section A** is filed the **final accounts,** followed by the **draft accounts**. Draft accounts become final after they are explained to the client and they are acceptable. If they were not acceptable then amendments have to be made.

In **Section B** is filed the completion notes. You find notes for the partner who is to review the accounts, notes of the meeting with the client, and the partners review points.

In **Section C** is filed the Tax computations if its a limited company. Tax computations for a sole trader and partnership are filed on their personal accounts.

In **Section D** is filed the details of repairs and renewals, plus sundry expenses. Tax inspectors are always particular about these expenses.

Client .... File No.............................
ACCOUNTS FOR THE YEAR ENDED............. STAFF.............................

A General		J Creditors	
1 ☐ Final Accounts		1 ☐ Lead Schedule	
2 ☐ Draft Accounts		2 ☐ Trade Creditors	
B Completion		3 ☐ Accruals	
1 ☐ Partner Review Points		4 ☐ HP Account	
2 ☐ Notes of Meeting		5 ☐ Other Loans	
3 ☐ Points for Partner		6 ☐ Other Creditors	
4 ☐ Review Points		7 ☐ Purchases Control	
5 ☐ Budget		**L Capital Accounts**	
C Taxation		1 ☐ Lead Schedule	
1 ☐ Tax Computations		2 ☐ Capital Introduced	
D Profit and Loss		3 ☐ Drawings	
1 ☐ Repairs/renewals		4 ☐ Tax Paid	
2 ☐ Sundry Expenses		**M Wages**	
E Fixed Assets		1 ☐ Wages Control	
1 ☐ Summary		2 ☐ PAYE & NI Control	
2 ☐ Additions		3 ☐ Wages Summary	
3 ☐ Disposals		**N Trial Balance**	
F Investments		1 ☐ Trial Balance	
1 ☐ Summary		2 ☐ Nominal Ledger	
2 ☐ Additions		3 ☐ Journal Adjustments	
3 ☐ Disposals		**O Vat**	
G Stock and Work in Progress		1 ☐ Vat Control	
☐		2 ☐ Vat Summary	
H Debtors		3 ☐ Reconciliation	
1 ☐ Lead Shedule			
2 ☐ Trade Debtors			
3 ☐ Prepayments			
4 ☐ Other Debtors			
5 ☐ Sales Control			
I Cash and Bank			
1 ☐ Lead Shedule			
2 ☐ Bank Control			
3 ☐ Bank Receipts			
4 ☐ Bank Payments			
5 ☐ Deposit Account			
6 ☐ Bank Loans			
7 ☐ Cash Account			
8 ☐ Cash Receipts			
9 ☐ Cash Payments			

In **Section E** is filed the fixed assets information. You find details of fixed assets bought, and those sold during the year.

There is a summary showing which fixed assets are in the business, their cost at the start and end of year.

You find the accumulated depreciation at the start of year, the depreciation charge for the year, and the accumulated depreciation by the end of the year.

You also find the net book value at the start, and at the end of year.

In **Section F** is filed information on other investments made by the business.

In **Section G** is filed the stock taking papers and computations, plus the work in progress.

Section H starts with a summary of the different types of debtors, and the totals as they appear on the balance sheet. Besides each figure, we write the reference page where it was computed.

Next is the list of trade debtors and the amount owed by each.

Next is a list of prepayments and how the figures were computed.

This is followed by a list of the other debtors. This includes those lent money by the business, or an insurance claim that is due soon.

Lastly, its the sales or debtors control account. This is where we find totals of what was sold on credit, what the debtors paid, and the total they still owe. The balance should be the same as the total on the list of debtors.

Section I starts with a schedule showing the different balances of cash, bank, bank loans, and credit card debts. Its followed by the bank control account, an annual summary of the banking, and an annual summary for the payments.

These are followed by the loan control account, the cash control account. We also file the cash receipts summary, and cash payments summary. Next is the credit card control account.

Section J starts with a list of the different types of creditors and the totals. This includes amounts owed for

VAT, plus the **PAYE** and **NI** contributions. A filing reference is indicated for the computations.

Next is a list of the different trade creditors and the total owed to each.

This is followed by a list of accrued expenses. We may attach the respective invoices which came in late.

Next is the hire purchase control account showing the source of the different figures.

This is followed by the creditors control account. It shows totals of what was bought on credit, what was paid, and the balance. The source of figures is indicated.

Section L is for capital in the business. It shows how the capital figure on the balance sheet is generated. There is a separate page for capital introduced during the year, as well as a page showing the drawings made in the year.

Section M starts with the wages control account. We have a page for **PAYE** and **NI** control account. It shows the national insurance and taxes deducted from employees. It shows what was paid to **Inland Revenue,** and what is outstanding. We have a wages summary, and pages with the detailed computations.

In **section N** we file the journal adjustments. If there are ledger accounts and a trial balance, they are filed in this section.

Section O starts with the VAT control account. We have a page with a summary of the input and output VAT. We also have a page reconciling the outstanding VAT at the year end.

Each of the pages is given an identification which is the filing reference. This is what we use to trace the source of figures used in the accounts.

For example the bank control account is I 2. This means its filed in **section I** and its the second one, just after I 1. In addition to this, we record initials of the staff member who prepared it, and the date it was done.

However, this file is the property of the accounting firm. In case tax inspectors want to know how accounts were prepared, this is what they ask for, plus the bookkeeping records.

Chapter 7

YEAR END PROCEDURES

This chapter explains how the accounting phase takes over from bookkeeping. How analysis books are summarised and annual control accounts are prepared.

At the end of a financial year or the 12 months, a summary of what was received and paid out is prepared. Various summaries are made for the monthly or quarterly periods in preparation for annual control accounts.

All the working papers generated are filed and cross referenced as explained in chapter 6.

The layout of the annual is similar to the monthly record. The only difference is that we only pick up totals from the monthly or quarterly periods.

THE RECEIPTS ANALYSIS SUMMARY

A summary of the receipts analysis for all the periods of the year is prepared. If the detailed analysis was done on a quarterly basis, we end up with only four different totals. However, in our business scenario bookkeeping was done monthly, so we end up with 12 totals as illustrated on the following page.

New Fashions   I 4

Receipts Analysis Summary - Monthly

April 2006 to March 2007

Month	Receipt Methods		Receipts Classification			
	Cash	Banking	Takings	Deposits	Interest	Loans
Apr	3,157.17	4,611.07	3,157.17	1,600.00	11.07	3,000.00
May	3,062.90	1,860.00	3,062.90	1,860.00		
Jun	3,342.20	2,050.00	3,342.20	2,050.00		
Jul	3,485.00	2,370.00	3,485.00	2,370.00		
Aug	3,606.85	1,350.00	3,606.85	1,350.00		
Sep	3,896.25	3,944.17	3,896.25	3,940.00	4.17	
Oct	3,946.65	2,660.40	3,946.65	2,650.00	10.40	
Nov	3,412.95	1,427.79	3,412.95	1,420.00	7.79	
Dec	3,312.05	2,873.62	3,312.05	2,860.00	13.62	
Jan	3,507.55	2,313.71	3,507.55	2,295.00	18.71	
Feb	3,757.25	2,937.37	3,757.25	2,910.00	27.37	
Mar	3,604.75	2,258.74	3,604.75	2,225.00	33.74	
	42,091.57	30,656.87	42,091.57	27,530.00	126.87	3,000.00

Receipt Methods   72,748.44

Receipts Classification   72,748.44

All these figures are just copied from the monthly receipts analyses prepared earlier on. Since they are not bulky, we file a copy in order to show where the monthly figures are extracted from.

We copy the monthly totals from the cash and banking columns. We also copy the monthly totals for takings, deposits, interest, and loans. After copying we get totals for each column.

The next step is verifying if what is recorded and added is correct. We add the cash and banking annual totals to get the total for receipt methods. In this case the answer is £72,748.44.

We also add the annual totals for takings, deposits, interest, and loans, in order to get the total for the receipts classification. The answer we get is £72,748.44.

Since the two totals are the same, we continue knowing what was copied and added are correct.

In our example, this receipts analysis summary is filed on the accounts file as I 4.

THE PAYMENTS ANALYSIS SUMMARY

A summary of the payments analyses is prepared for the 12 months as illustrated on the following pages.

General Knowledge   Bookkeeping   &   Accounts

New Fashions   **April 2006 to March 2007**

Payment Analysis Summary

	Payment Methods			Payment Analysis Columns														
Month	Cash	Bank	Credit card	Purchases	Direct Expenses	Salaries & Wages	Premises Costs	Repairs & Maintenance	Gen Admin	Motor Expenses	Legal & Profesional	Bank & finance charges	Interest Charges	Sundry Expenses	FA above £100	Drawings	Credit card repaymt	Loan repaymt
April	1,166.66	2,710.73	256.65	2,503.33	15.00	346.66	260.00	-	16.75	-	-	11.95	12.50	18.40	-	568.80	256.65	125.00
May	1,310.36	4,704.22	257.95	1,561.73	-	346.66	260.00	-	19.15	-	-	19.50	18.74	-	3,000.00	708.80	257.95	125.00
June	1,166.66	1,980.25	302.92	1,599.25	-	346.66	260.00	-	22.95	-	-	21.27	17.98	-	185.00	568.80	302.92	125.00
July	1,173.16	2,458.40	326.27	2,243.23	-	346.66	260.00	-	24.38	-	-	20.08	18.81	24.60	-	708.80	326.27	125.00
August	1,306.66	1,839.74	315.14	1,574.68	-	346.66	260.00	29.50	21.36	-	-	11.81	23.59	45.00	-	568.80	315.14	125.00
September	1,166.66	1,968.46	226.77	1,734.79	-	346.66	260.00	-	18.94	55.20	-	13.23	12.50	-	-	568.80	226.77	125.00
October	965.20	1,403.29	270.67	865.70	-	346.66	260.00	-	25.39	-	-	24.44	12.50	-	-	708.80	270.67	125.00
November	1,166.66	1,941.38	130.46	1,540.78	39.50	346.66	260.00	-	16.48	-	150.00	22.12	12.50	26.20	-	568.80	130.46	125.00
December	1,166.66	1,694.43	115.30	1,394.03	-	346.66	260.00	-	16.00	115.30	-	23.80	12.50	-	-	568.80	115.30	125.00
January	1,306.66	1,276.51	245.54	1,087.87	-	346.66	260.00	-	25.55	-	-	16.79	12.50	-	-	708.80	245.54	125.00
February	1,173.86	1,178.71	23.75	963.97	-	346.66	260.00	-	29.37	-	-	22.52	12.50	23.75	-	568.80	23.75	125.00
March	1,166.66	950.82	66.30	681.79	-	346.66	260.00	-	36.98	66.30	-	19.45	12.50	-	-	568.80	66.30	125.00
	40,930.51																	
Paymt methods	14,235.86	24,106.95	2,587.71	17,706.15	54.50	4,159.92	3,120.00	29.50	271.30	236.80	150.00	226.96	179.12	137.95	3,185.00	7,365.60	2,587.71	1,500.00
Total Paymts	40,930.51																	
	I 9	I 2	I 12	A 2	A 2	A 2	A 2	A 2	A 2	A 2	A 2	A 2	I 8	A 2	E 1	A 2	I 12	I 7

Since this complete illustration is so small, its expanded and split it into two, on the following page.

New Fashions — April 2006 to March 2007

Payment Analysis Summary

Payment Methods

Month	Cash	Bank	Credit card	Purchases	Direct Expenses	Salaries & Wages	Premises Costs	Repairs & Maintenanc
April	1,166.66	2,710.73	256.65	2,503.33	15.00	346.66	260.00	-
May	1,310.36	4,704.22	257.95	1,516.73	-	346.66	260.00	-
June	1,166.66	1,980.25	302.92	1,599.25	-	346.66	260.00	-
July	1,173.16	2,458.40	326.27	2,243.23	-	346.66	260.00	-
August	1,306.66	1,839.74	315.14	1,574.68	-	346.66	260.00	29.50
September	1,166.66	1,968.46	226.77	1,734.79	-	346.66	260.00	-
October	965.20	1,403.29	270.67	865.70	-	346.66	260.00	-
November	1,166.66	1,941.38	180.46	1,540.78	39.50	346.66	260.00	-
December	1,166.66	1,694.43	115.30	1,394.03	-	346.66	260.00	-
January	1,306.66	1,276.51	245.54	1,087.87	-	346.66	260.00	-
February	1,173.86	1,178.71	23.75	963.97	-	346.66	260.00	-
March	1,166.66	950.82	66.30	681.79	-	346.66	260.00	-
Paymt methods	40,930.51	14,235.86	24,106.95	2,587.71	17,706.16	54.50	4,159.92	3,120.00	29.50
Total paymts	40,930.51								
		I 9	I 2	I 12	A 2	A 2	A 2	A 2	A 2

I 5

Payment Analysis Columns

Gen Admin	Motor Expenses	Legal & Profesional	Bank & finance charges	Interest Charges	Sundry Expenses	FA above £100	Drawings	Credit card repaymt	Loan repaymt
15.75	-	-	11.95	12.50	18.40	-	568.80	256.65	125.00
19.15	-	-	19.50	18.74	-	3,000.00	708.80	257.95	125.00
22.95	-	-	21.27	17.98	-	185.00	568.80	302.92	125.00
24.38	-	-	20.08	18.81	24.60	-	568.80	326.27	125.00
21.36	-	-	11.81	23.59	45.00	-	708.80	315.14	125.00
18.94	55.20	-	13.23	12.50	-	-	568.80	226.77	125.00
25.39	-	-	24.44	12.50	-	-	708.80	270.67	125.00
16.48	-	150.00	22.12	12.50	26.20	-	568.80	180.46	125.00
15.00	115.30	-	23.80	12.50	-	-	568.80	115.30	125.00
25.55	-	-	16.79	12.50	-	-	708.80	245.54	125.00
29.37	-	-	22.52	12.50	23.75	-	568.80	23.75	125.00
36.98	66.30	-	19.45	12.50	-	-	568.80	66.30	125.00
271.30	236.80	150.00	226.96	179.12	137.95	3,185.00	7,385.60	2,587.71	1,500.00
A 2	A 2	A 2	A 2	I 8	A 2	E 1	A 2	I 12	I 7

These totals are picked up from the 12 monthly payment analyses. The totals for each column are calculated to get the annual figures.

However, the verification here is done using cross casts only. We add the cash, bank and credit card totals. We also add the totals for all the payment analysis columns. The sums for the two calculations should be the same. In this case we have £40,930.51 for both, and we can go ahead. This is shown on the half illustrated at the top on the previous page.

We do indicate where the figures come from. A copy of the monthly or quarterly detailed payment analyses are filed as well. In our example, this payments summary is filed as I 5.

THE BANK CONTROL ACCOUNT

After the separate summaries, the annual control accounts are prepared. The aim is to verify the annual bookkeeping records against independent sources of information.

What is recorded is verified, against the balance on the last bank statement for the year. So a bank control account is prepared. We have an illustration on the following page.

New Fashions				12
Bank Control Account				
April 2006 to March 2007				
		Value In	**Value Out**	
		Receipts	Payments	Balance
Balance b/d				325.00
Banking	14	30,656.87		
Paymts	15		24,106.95	
		30,656.87	24,106.95	**6,874.93**

The opening balance of £325 is extracted from the balance sheet for the previous year. Total banking is picked up from the receipts analysis summary.

Besides the £30,656.87 is written the filing reference where the figure is generated. This is the annual receipts analysis summary filed as **14**. In this book its on page 34.

The total payments figure of £24,106.95 is extracted from the annual payments summary. Besides this figure is the filing reference **15**, where it was derived. In this book its on page 36 and 37.

The closing balance is got by adding total receipts to the opening balance, and deducting total payments. To prove the £6,874.93 is correct, it should be the same as the balance on the control account for the last month or quarter of the year.

This should also be the same as the bank statement balance at the year end.

On the accounts file, this control account would be filed as **I2.**

Since the bookkeeping information is extracted from bank statements, and there are no unpresented cheques at the year end, there is no need for bank reconciliation.

Bank reconciliation is an explanation provided, to account for the difference between the balance on the bank control account, and the balance on the bank statement for the same period.

THE LOAN CONTROL ACCOUNT

The Loan control account is prepared to verify what is recorded, by comparing with the last loan statement for the year.

It summarises the loan amount received, interest due, amount paid back, and charges for the year. On the following page is an illustration.

New Fashions   I 6

Bank Loan Control Account

April 2006 to March 2007

		Receipts	Payments	Balance
Balance b/d				-
Principle	I 7	3,000		
First Year Interest	I 7	150		
Principle repaid	I 5		1,500	
Interest Paid	I 8		150	
		3,150	1,650	**1,500**

In the receipts column is the total borrowed from the bank and interest due for the first year. These are extracted from the loan agreement and a copy is filed as I7.

In the payments column is a total of the principle loan paid back. The reference page for the detail is I5.

We also have the total interest paid. However, this figure is mixed up with overdraft interest on I5. So the interest on the loan is isolated on a separate page filed as I8. This is illustrated on the following page.

The loan balance at the year end is equal to amount received, plus interest due, less total payments for the year.

To confirm that records are correct, the control account balance of £1,500 should be the same as the one on the last loan statement for the year.

On the accounts file, this control account would be filed as **I6.**

New Fashions   I 8

April 2006 to March 2007

Loan and Overdraft Interest Isolated

Month	Total Interest	Loan Interest	Overdraft Interest
Apr-06	12.50	12.50	
May-06	18.74	12.50	6.24
Jun-06	17.98	12.50	5.48
Jul-06	18.81	12.50	6.31
Aug-06	23.59	12.50	11.09
Sep-06	12.50	12.50	
Oct-06	12.50	12.50	
Nov-06	12.50	12.50	
Dec-06	12.50	12.50	
Jan-07	12.50	12.50	
Feb-07	12.50	12.50	
Mar-07	12.50	12.50	
	179.12	150.00	29.12

I 6

The two types of interest are separated by extracting the monthly details. We then record them in the respective columns. The monthly and annual totals do not change.

Please note that besides the £150 on **I6,** its written **I8.** This indicates where the £150 was computed. Below the £150 on **I8** above, its written **I6.** This indicates where the computed £150 is utilised.

THE CASH CONTROL ACCOUNT

The cash control account shows the total cash received and paid out during the year. It helps to confirm if the records are correct, by comparing its balance with the total cash available in form of notes and coins.

It also helps to know how much should be in the cash till. This is important where personal and business money is mixed up.

Below is an illustration;

New Fashions				I 9
Cash Control Account				
April 2006 to March 2007				
		Value In	**Value Out**	
		Receipts	Payments	Balance
Balance b/d				124.00
Takings	I 10	42,091.57		
Deposits	I 4		27,530.00	
Paymts	I 5		14,235.86	
		42,091.57	41,765.86	**449.71**

It starts with the opening balance of £124, available at the start of year.

Next is the total cash received of £42,091.57. Its

picked up from the Receipts Analysis Summary filed as I4. In this book its on page 34.

The deposits figure of £27,530 is extracted from the same Receipts Analysis summary, filed as **I4.**

The total payments figure of £14,235.86 is extracted from the annual payments summary filed as **I5.** In this book its on page 36 to 37.

The closing balance is got by adding total receipts to the opening balance, and deducting total payments.

To prove its correct, it should be the same as the balance on the cash control account for the 12th month. It should also be the value of notes and coins on the last day of the financial year.

On the accounts file, this control account would be filed as **I9.**

CREDIT CARD CONTROL ACCOUNT

A control account is prepared for credit card transactions, to confirm if the records agree with the last credit card statement for the year. On the following page is an illustration;

New Fashions   I 12

Credit Card Control Account

April 2006 to March 2007

		Value In	Value Out	
		Receipts	Payments	Balance
Balance b/d				-
Borrowed	I 5	2,587.71		
Paid back	I 5		2,587.71	
Interest Paid				-
		2,587.71	2,587.71	-

In this case there is no opening balance.

In the receipts column is a total of £2,587.71. This is what the business received from the credit card company. And its what the credit card company paid on behalf of the business.

Its extracted from the payments summary that is filed as I5. In this book its on page 36 and 37. Its just next to the bank payments total among the payment methods. Below it, is written I12. This is the filing reference where the figure is used, on the above control account.

In the payments column is a total of £2,587.71 paid back to the credit card company. Its extracted from the same payments analysis summary filed as I5. Its the total of the credit card repayment column.

Since the whole amount was paid back in full, there is no balance and there is no debt. There is no interest since the monthly totals were paid back within the interest free period of 50 days.

The balance is zero and its the same as the one on the last credit card statement received for the year. If there are any differences, they are investigated and corrections made.

In the top right hand corner of this control account is written I12. That is the filing reference on the accounts file. Next to this is written the staff Initials and the date it was prepared.

A copy of the last credit card statement is filed to prove the balance

.

Chapter 8

ADJUSTMENTS

This chapter explains what adjustments are. Why some payments and receipts are excluded, and others added. It also considers what the business has at the start and end of year.

Adjustments are additions and subtractions made to summarised bookkeeping records, in order to prepare final accounts according to the regulations.

Before preparing accounts, we scrutinise all the control accounts. In addition to what is recorded and summarised, we look out for what is not yet recorded.

If the business has credit transactions, we look out for outstanding debtors and creditors. Since our scenario is a cash business, we just look out for unrecorded receipts and invoices, which were received after the year end.

At this stage we isolate income from receipts, and isolate expenses from payments in order to prepare the profit and loss account.

RECEIPTS AND INCOME

All money received in the business is recorded as receipts. This includes sales, takings, commission, capital, loans, and others. However, to prepare the profit and loss account, we only use income.

Income is that money received from the sale of goods and services by the business.

Money received from the owner is capital, and not an income.

Borrowed money is not income, its a liability or debt to the business.

INCOME ADJUSTMENTS

After isolating income from the rest, we may need to deduct what doesn't belong to that financial year.

Income in advance is the one received for a period that is beyond the financial year end. This is excluded from accounts for the recent year, by deducting it from the rest. Its recorded on the balance sheet as a current liability.

Income due is income that wasn't recorded in the bookkeeping records. Its rare that there is need to add to the income already received or invoiced.

PAYMENTS AND EXPENSES

Not all payments made are recognized as expenses, when preparing a profit and loss account. We have four classifications as explained on the following page.

1. The first are personal payments known as **drawings**. These are recorded separately in the drawings column and are not recognized as business expenses. They are not recorded on the profit and loss account since they are personal. They are recorded on the balance sheet.

2. **Fixed assets** are not business expenses since they are used for many years. Their value lost or used up in the year is calculated as **depreciation**. Its only the depreciation value which is recorded on the profit and loss account.

3. **Liabilities** or debts repaid are not expenses. In this case we have a loan and credit card repayments.

4. All the other payments made for the business' requirements are accepted as **expenses** for the profit and loss account.

Among these expenses we have the cost of buying what was sold. That is what we record as **purchases**. We have expenses incurred directly in relation to what was sold. We record them as **direct expenses**. The rest are known as **overhead expenses.**

DEPRECIATION

The cost of a fixed asset is written off to the profit and loss account as **depreciation.**

However, if the asset is to last 3 years, its cost is not all written off in the year of purchase. The cost is divided up among the 3 years, to get the value to write off in each year.

The easiest way of deriving depreciation is by; divide the cost of the asset, by the number of years its to be used. This is known as the **straight line method.** There are other methods of calculating like the **reducing balance method**.

Calculations for depreciation are made separately for each category of fixed assets. On the following page is an illustration.

We start by recording the **opening balances** in the cost, depreciation, and net book value sections. Those are the values available on the 1st of April 2006.

Next we **add the cost** of fixed assets bought during the year, and **deduct those**

sold. In this example, we add the van and storage unit bought. This leads us to the original cost of all fixed assets available at the year end.

Next is **calculating the depreciation charge for the year.** In our example we use the straight line method. Since the car (£3,000) is estimated to last 4 years, the annual depreciation is £750.

The depreciation on furniture and fittings available at the beginning of the year is £120, since the opening value of £240 was to last another 2 years.

The storage unit is to last two years. So the £185 is divided by two, giving £92.50 per year. So the total is £212.50 for all furniture and fittings.

New Fashions

April 2006 to March 2007

Fixed Assets Summary

	COST				DEPRECIATION				NET BOOK VALUE	
	Cost 1-Apr-06	Addi tions	Disp osals	Cost 31-Mar-07	Depn 1-Apr-06	Disp osals	Chrge for Yr	Depn 31-Mar-07	NBV 1-Apr-06	NBV 31-Mar-07
Motor Vehicles										
VW Van	-	3,000.00		3,000.00	0.00		750.00	750.00	0	2,250.00
Fixtures & Fittings	360.00	185.00		545.00	120.00		212.50	332.50	240	212.50
	360.00	**3,185.00**	-	**3,545.00**	**120.00**	-	**962.50**	**1,082.50**	**240.00**	**2,462.50**

Next is getting the accumulated depreciation to date, by adding the opening depreciation to the charge for the year. The figure for motor vehicles is £750, while the one for furniture and fittings is £332.50

Next is getting the net book value at the year end. We deduct total depreciation from total cost. We use the values at the 31st of March 2007. The figure for motor vehicles is £2,250, while the one for furniture and fittings is £212.50.

The simple verification of figures here is by adding the net book value to total depreciation, to see if we get the cost figure.

The figures we use on the balance sheet is the net book value.

The page on which all this depreciation calculation is done, is filed in **section E** on the accounts file.

PREPAYMENTS

These are expenses paid for a month or period that is beyond the financial year. In our scenario, the financial year ends on 31st March 2007. They are also known as **payments in advance.**

If an insurance payment is made and the policy expires on the 30th of April. The amount for April is said to have been paid in advance.

So the April payment is calculated and excluded, by

deducting it from the total insurance payment.

All payments in advance are deducted, leaving only those expenses that relate to the financial year in question.

All prepayments are listed, totaled, and filed in **section H** on the accounts file.

Although that money is already paid, its not yet spent. So its still an asset to the business, for one or a few more months. This is why its recorded among the current assets on the balance sheet.

ACCRUED EXPENSES

These are expenses which were not yet recorded by the year end. One of the reasons is, the bill was not yet received. These bills are normally received within the next 30 days after the year end.

So the prepared accounts are not finalized before this period expires. They constitute part of **what is not in the bookkeeping records.**

Examples are phone and electricity bills. Since the Accountant's invoice for preparing these accounts is not yet recorded in the bookkeeping, their fees are also outstanding by the year end date.

So the **unrecorded expense amounts** are **added** to the total in their category, when preparing the profit and loss account.

For example, the unrecorded phone bill is added to the total phone bill already accumulated for the year.

The reasoning is, the expense was incurred within the financial year, its only the bill which was received late. It could be due to a postal strike.

The expense is recognized in the financial year but the payment is not yet done. So all accrued expenses are listed on a separate sheet that is filed in **section J** on the accounts file.

Their total is recorded on the balance sheet among current liabilities. These are debts to be repaid within the next 12 months.

BAD DEBTS

This happens to those who sell on credit and their customers eventually don't pay. If debt recovery procedures fail, a decision is made to write it off as a bad debt.

A total is computed for all bad debts, and recorded on the profit and loss account among the expenses.

Its deducted from gross profit and it reduces net profit, as indicated in the next chapter.

So the balance of debtors recorded on the balance sheet is also reduced.

CLOSING STOCK

This is stock not yet sold by the year end date. All items are listed and counted.

The number of units for each item are multiplied by their **cost price.** The resulting figures are added to get the closing stock value.

This figure is used on both the profit and loss account, and balance sheet.

OPENING BALANCES

This is a list of values showing assets, liabilities, and capital extracted from the balance sheet for the previous year. The closing balances for a previous year, are the opening balances for the year we prepare accounts for. We can refer to this as an **opening balance sheet.**

If we are preparing the very first accounts for a particular business, there isn't a previous year balance sheet.

Instead there is an **opening statement**. Its contents and those of an opening balance sheet are the same.

On the following page is an illustration.

New Fashions

Balance Sheet
For the Year Ended 31 March 2006

Fixed Assets		
Furniture and Fittings		240.00
		240.00
Current Assets		
Stock	1,150.00	
Bank	325.00	
Cash	124.00	
	1,599.00	
Current Liabilites	0	
Net current assets		1,599.00
Net Assets		**1,839.00**
Financed By		
Capital		1,839.00
Total Financing		**1,839.00**

These are the assets, liabilities and capital the business had at the start of the financial year.

The furniture and fittings value is used to calculate depreciation for the profit and loss account, plus its net book value for the balance sheet.

The stock figure is what we refer to as **opening stock.** Its used when preparing the profit and loss account.

The bank figure is used as the opening balance on the bank control account for the year.

The cash figure is used as the opening balance on the cash control account for the year.

The capital figure is used on the balance sheet at the year end.

If there is no opening balance sheet but an opening statement, it has to balance. The total financing should be equal to the net assets figure.

On the previous page illustration, both the total financing and the net assets figure are £1,839.

JOURNALS

A Journal is a recording for an adjustment that is to be made in the accounts. Journals are made after the summaries and control accounts have been done. They indicate the amounts, where they are recorded, and why.

An example is an **accrued expense** like the Accountant's fees. This is illustrated below;

Journal Number	Detail	Debit	Credit
1	Accountancy Fees- Profit & Loss Ac	1,250	
	Accruals - Balance sheet		1,250
	Accountancy Fees for the year		

The journal says that £1,250 is Accountancy fees, which is recorded as an expense on the profit and loss account. Expenses are recorded in the **debit column,** while incomes are recorded in the credit column.

The second £1,250 is recorded as an accrual among the current liabilities on the balance sheet. Liabilities are recorded in the **credit column**, while assets are recorded in the debit column.

Below these **figures** is a **narration** which provides some explanation about the transaction. On this journal it says "Accountancy fees for the year".

So the record where an adjustments is introduced in the accounts is a journal.

A Journal is made for each adjustment. Each of them is numbered, and the filing reference for the source document is indicated. Journals are filed in **section N** on the accounts file.

Chapter 9

THE PROFIT AND LOSS ACCOUNT

This chapter explains the purpose of a profit and loss account. What information is used to prepare it, and the procedure followed.

After summarising all the bookkeeping records, verifying using control accounts, and preparing the adjustments, next we prepare a trading profit and loss account.

This account is prepared to establish if the business made a profit or a loss from its trading activities. We start with a draft and that is where we write the filing reference for all the figures used.

The draft is presented and explained to the client. If its accepted we go ahead to prepare the final accounts. On the following page is an illustration;

Its started with income and in this case its **sales** which is copied from the cash control account. The amount is £42,091.57. The filing reference for the source is I9. In this book its on page 43.

The **opening stock** comes from the opening balances and the cross reference is **N1**. In this book its on page 56. The amount is £1,150.

New Fashions   **A 2**

Trading, Profit And Loss Account
For the Year Ended 31 March 2007

Sales	I 9		42,091.57
Opening Stock	N 1	1,150.00	
Purchases	I 5	17,706.16	
Direct Expenses		54.50	
		18,910.66	
Closing Stock	G 1	-1,420.00	
Cost of Sales			-17,490.66
Gross Profit			**24,600.91**
Interest Received	I 4		126.87
			24,727.78

Overhead Expenses

Salaries & Wages,	I 5	4,159.92	
Premises Costs	I 5	3,120.00	
Repairs & Maintenance	I 5	29.50	
Gen Administration	I 5	271.30	
Motor Expenses	I 5	236.80	
Accountancy Fees	N 2	1,250.00	
Legal & Professional	I 5	150.00	
Bank charges	I 5	226.96	
Interest	I 5	179.12	
Sundry Expenses	I 5	137.95	
Depreciation	E 1	962.50	
Total Overheads			10,724.05
Net Profit			**14,003.73**

The **purchases** figure is taken from the payments analysis summary filed as **I5**. In this book its on page 36 and 37 The amount is £17,706.16.

Direct expenses is also taken from the payments analysis summary. The amount is £54.50.

Closing stock is derived from stock taking and the filling reference is **G1**. The amount is £1,420.

Opening stock plus purchases, plus direct expenses, less closing stock, gives the **cost of sales**. The figure is £17,490.66. Its the cost of what was sold.

Cost of sales is deducted from sales to get the **gross profit**. This is the difference between the selling price and the cost of what was sold. The figure is £24,600.91.

There is a separate type of income, **Interest Received**, which is not related to what was sold. The amount is £126.87. Its added to gross profit before deducting expenses. The amount we get is £24,727.78, and it's the net income.

Next is listing all the **overhead expenses** extracted from the same payments analysis summary.

Exceptional references are for adjustments which are filed in **section N**.

Prepayments are deducted, while accrued expenses are added to their respective totals. In this case the only accrual is the Accountant's fees.

Depreciation is also listed among the overhead expenses. The figure is £962.50 and its filing reference is **E1.**

Next is getting the **total overhead expenditure.** The figure in our illustration is £10,724.05.

The total overheads are deducted from net income to get **net profit.** If there is no other type of income, total overheads are deducted from gross profit.

The figure got for net profit is £14,003.74. If the overhead expenses are more than gross profit then its a **net loss.**

Net profit is the reward to the owners for having risked by investing their money or resources. They also put in a lot of effort to ensure the business succeeds.

If its a net loss, its equivalent to the invested amount that is lost in the business.

The net profit or loss is used on the balance sheet.

After discussing the draft with the client and making the necessary changes, we prepare the final Trading, Profit and Loss account.

On the final copy, we add comparative figures for the previous year. This is illustrated on the following page.

The filing reference for the source of figures ends with the draft copy.

New Fashions A 1

Trading, Profit And Loss Account
For the Year Ended 31 March 2007

	2007		2006	
Sales		42,091.57		39,457.92
Opening Stock	1,150.00		985.88	
Purchases	17,706.16		16,549.74	
Direct Expenses	54.50		74.70	
	18,910.66		17,610.32	
Closing Stock	-1,420.00		1,150.00	
Cost of Sales		-17,490.66		-18,760.32
Gross Profit		24,600.91		20,697.60
Interest Received		126.87		94.70
		24,727.78		20,792.30
Expenses				
Salaries & Wages,	4,159.92		3,743.93	
Premises Costs	3,120.00		2,808.00	
Repairs & Maintenance	29.50		26.55	
Gen Administration	271.30		244.17	
Motor Expenses	236.80		213.12	
Accountancy Fees	1,250.00		1,125.00	
Legal & Professional	150.00		135.00	
Bank charges	226.96		204.26	
Interest	179.12		161.21	
Sundry Expenses	137.95		124.16	
Depreciation	962.50		120.00	
Total Overheads		10,724.05		8,905.40
Net Profit		14,003.73		11,886.91

This presentation gives the user an opportunity to compare with the figures for the previous year.

Final Accounts are more informative when there are some figures to compare with.

According to the above illustration, we can see an increase in sales, from £39,457.92 to £42,091.57. The gross profit and net profit increased as compared to the previous year.

There is an increase in all expense categories except the direct expenses which dropped by about £20.00.

Before compiling ratios as explained in chapter 13, one is able to make some comparison using the raw figures themselves.

Chapter 10

THE BALANCE SHEET

This chapter explains what a balance sheet is. What information is used to prepare it, and the procedure followed.

A Balance Sheet is a statement which shows what a business owns in form of assets, what it owes in form of liabilities, capital contributed by owners, and the accumulated profits.

Assets are the items owned by a business, and are classified into current and fixed assets.

Fixed assets are items bought for use in the business for several years. Examples are fixtures and fittings, motor vehicles, equipment, land and buildings, plus goodwill. All these are commonly known except goodwill.

Goodwill is a share of future profits that was paid to the previous owner of a business. This value is set by the previous owner at the time of selling. Its only endorsed on the balance sheet when the buyer pays for it.

The argument is that they used resources to raise the profit generating ability of the business. The business and the goodwill cannot be separated. So if a business is being sold, the buyer must pay the value attached to goodwill, in addition to the other net assets being sold.

Since goodwill is a lump sum pay off of future profit, to a previous owner. When the profit is actually made, what was paid to the previous owner is deducted. This is what we call **Goodwill amortization**.

The goodwill is deducted, together with the expenses, and we end up with a reduced net profit figure. By this, we are allocating some

of the current profits to the previous owner.

So the amortization is done for a number of years until the goodwill is totally written off, and it disappears from the balance sheet.

Current assets are those whose form is constantly changed in order to make profit, and to sustain the business. They include; stock, debtors, bank balance and cash. Below is an illustration of how their form keeps on changing;

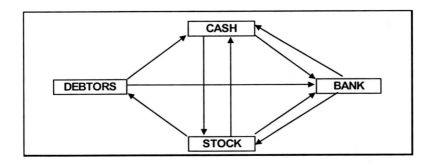

The form of cash changes to stock when products are bought for resale. When stock is sold for a cheque its form changes to bank. If stock is sold on credit it becomes debtors. When debtors pay cash their form changes to cash.

Other current assets are **prepayments** or expenses paid in advance. They are treated as money which still belongs to the business. It ceases to belong in the following year, when the period paid for has passed. In that year is when its transferred to the profit and loss account, as part of the expenses.

A liability is money owed by a business. They are classified into current and long term.

A long-term liability is borrowed money or assets bought on credit, and are repaid in a period that exceeds one year. Examples are bank loans and assets bought by hire purchase.

A current liability is a debt to be repaid in a period of 12 months. Examples are accrued expenses, creditors, and a bank overdraft.

Accruals are expenses which were not in the bookkeeping records by the balance sheet date.

Creditors refer to suppliers who are paid after 30 to 90 days. What we have on the balance sheet is a total of those outstanding by the balance sheet date.

A **bank overdraft** is a short term money borrowing facility provided by banks to current account holders. Its repaid back within 12 months. The balance outstanding is what we record among current liabilities.

The line of distinction is that current liabilities are repaid within a year, while long-term liabilities are repaid beyond 12 months.

Capital is the money or value of what the owners contribute to a business. Its the one which finances or pays for the net assets in a business.

However, capital can also be borrowed. This is what we find as long-term liabilities. So a business is financed by capital and long-term liabilities.

On the following page is an illustration of a balance sheet.

The title is the client its prepared for, plus the financial year it covers.

Its started with **fixed assets** at their net book value, and they are summed up. In this case we have motor vehicles plus fixtures and fittings. The filing reference where those figures are extracted from is **E1**. In this book you find those calculations on page 51. Their total is £2,462.50.

Next are the **current assets**. The filing reference for the source of each of those figures is indicated as **G1, I2, and I9**. In this book **I2** is on page 39, while **I9** is on page 43. Their total is £8,744.64.

New Fashions   A 2

Balance Sheet
For the Year Ended 31 March 2007

Fixed Assets			
Furniture and Fittings	E 1		212.50
Motor Vehicles	E 1		2,250.00
			2,462.50
Current Assets			
Stock	G 1	1,420.00	
Bank	I 2	6,874.93	
Cash	I 9	449.71	
		8,744.64	
Current Liabilites			
Accruals		- 1,250.00	
Net Current Assets			7,494.64
Net Assets			**9,957.14**
Financed By			
Loan	I 6		1,500.00
Capital at Start	N 1	1,839.00	
Profit	A 2	14,003.74	
		15,842.74	
Drawings	I 5	- 7,385.60	
Closing Capital			8,457.14
			9,957.14

Current assets are arranged in **order of liquidity.** This is where Stock is recorded first. The reason is its the least liquid, or takes longest to convert into cash. We end with cash which doesn't need any time to convert. Its already liquid.

Next are **current liabilities** and they are added up. In this case there are no creditors since they pay immediately. The only accruals is the Accountant's fees.

Current liabilities are deducted from current assets to get **net current assets,** if its a positive answer. In this case the figure is £7,494.64. If its a negative answer then its **net current liabilities**.

Net current assets (liabilities) are added to fixed assets to get **Net Assets.** This is the net value of what is owned by a business. In this case the figure is **£9,957.14.**

Next we have the **financing section**. This business is financed by a **loan** balance of £1,500, and **capital**.

The capital brought forward from the previous year was £1,839. We add net profit and deduct drawings. This gives the new capital figure in the business of £8,457.14.

So total financing in the business is **£9,957.14.** This figure is **equal** to the net assets value above. This is when the balance sheet is said to have balanced.

If it doesn't balance then there is an error and its not completed yet. The cause of difference must be investigated and corrected.

However, the layout of capital on this balance sheet is for a sole trader. The layout for a partnership and a limited company are different.

A sole trader is one who owns a business alone.

A partnership business is owned by between 2 and 20 people.

A limited company is owned by shareholders.

After discussing the draft with the client and making the necessary changes, we prepare the final Balance Sheet.

On the final copy, we add comparative figures for the previous year, and get rid of the filing references. This is illustrated on the following page.

This presentation gives the user an opportunity to compare with the figures for the previous year.

Final Accounts are more informative when there are some figures to compare with.

Before compiling the ratios, one is able to make some comparison using the raw figures themselves.

According to the balance sheet figures on the next page, the financial position of the business is much better than what it was at the end of the previous year.

The owner's capital increased from £1,839 to £8457.14.

The financing and net assets in the business are much higher in 2007, than what it was at the end the 2006 financial year.

More comparisons can be made using these balance sheet figures as explained in chapter 13.

New Fashions A 1

Balance Sheet
For the Year Ended 31 March 2007

	2007		2006	
Fixed Assets				
Furniture and Fittings		212.50		240.00
Motor Vehicles		2,250.00		-
		2,462.50		240.00
Current Assets				
Stock	1,420.00		1,150.00	
Bank	6,874.93		325.00	
Cash	449.71		124.00	
	8,744.64		1,599.00	
Current Liabilites				
Accruals	- 1,250.00		-	
Net Current Assets		7,494.64		1,599.00
Net Assets		**9,957.14**		**1,839.00**
Financed By				
Loan		1,500.00		-
Capital at Start	1,839.00		1,381.02	
Profit	14,003.74		11,886.91	
	15,842.74		13,267.93	
Drawings	- 7,385.60		- 11,428.93	
Closing Capital		8,457.14		1,839.00
		9,957.14		**1,839.00**

Chapter 11

NOTES TO THE ACCOUNTS

This chapter explains the notes attached to Accounts prepared for limited companies.

Notes are written statements which provide some explanation about the contents, and how the accounts were prepared.

They are required for limited companies, and not sole traders or partnerships. They are part of the accounts sent to the **Registrar of Companies.**

They do provide clarifications since there is more than one accepted method of preparing accounts. Below are some of the issues in the notes.

We mention the Accounting regulations being complied with, and the Accounting policies used. For example, we clarify if we used the straight line, or reducing balance method of depreciation, plus the percentages used.

We mention if Vat is included in the sales figure or not.

We disclose the emoluments or salaries paid to Directors.

We show the corporation tax computed and the percentage used.

Dividends due to shareholders in the company are also mentioned.

We show how the value of fixed assets on the balance sheet was computed. This summarises the computations we filed as **G1** on the Accounts file.

We show the cost, accumulated depreciation, and net book value at the beginning and end of year. We also show the depreciation charge for the year.

The different figures making up total debtors on the balance sheet are shown.

The different figures making up total creditors on the balance sheet are also shown.

We show how capital in the business is made up. How much is authorized, issued, and fully paid.

The value of transactions between directors and the business are disclosed.

A comprehensive Trading Profit and Loss Account is attached. The reason is; the one just before the balance sheet is so brief.

Chapter 12

WAGES, NIC AND TAXES

This chapter explains the treatment of wages, national insurance contributions, and taxes in the accounts. The adjustment of profits for tax purposes, and VAT are briefly look at.

WAGES

Accountants also provide a **payroll service** for businesses which employ people.

This involves computing tax and the National Insurance contributions deducted from each employee's pay. Clients are informed; how much net pay is due to employees, and how much PAYE tax and National Insurance to pay to Inland Revenue. This is the tax collecting Department of Government.

The wages cost on the profit and loss account is an addition of; net wages paid to employees, the taxes, and the National Insurance contributions paid to Inland Revenue.

In the scenario used in this book, no taxes or National Insurance contributions were deducted. The total paid to the single employee is below the starting threshold for taxes and National Insurance deductions.

So the wages cost on the profit and loss account is just equal to what was paid to the employee.

If the income for an employee exceeds £5,200 per year, the business is required by law, to deduct **PAYE tax and National Insurance contributions (NIC)**. This creates more work.

In addition to computing what is due to the Government, it has to be accounted for, and paid over to Government regularly.

The weekly or monthly wage, and deduction computations are put together to get an annual summary. After this we prepare the wages and the PAYE /NI control accounts.

All the working papers regarding wages are filed in **section N** on the Accounts file.

NET WAGES

The weekly or monthly net wages paid to employees are recorded on the net wages account.

Its called net wages since the PAYE tax and national insurance contributions have been deducted.

We have some figures on the following net wages account for illustration.

Please note; the figures are intentionally different from what we used in previous chapters. The ones used in previous chapters were below the starting threshold   for PAYE & NI deductions.

New Fashions

April 2006 to March 2007

Net Wages Account Summary

	Dr	Cr
April	564.93	
May	564.93	
June	564.93	
July	564.93	
August	564.93	
September	564.93	
October	564.93	
November	564.93	
December	564.93	
January	564.93	
February	564.93	
March	564.93	
To Gross Wages Account		6,779.16
	6,779.16	6,779.16

There is a net monthly wage of £564.93. These figures are extracted from the payments analysis. The total for the year is £6,779.16. Its transferred to the Gross Wages account at the year end.

Since there is no balance on this account, its figures are not recorded on the Profit and Loss account.

GROSS WAGES

Gross wages is the total cost of wages to the business. It's made up of the following; the net wages paid to employees, the **PAYE tax** and **NI** deducted from employees' pay, plus the employer's NI contribution.

The employer is required to contribute a certain amount in addition to the employee's NI deductions.

All the four components are recorded on the Gross Wages Account as illustrated below;

New Fashions

April 2006 to March 2007

Gross Wages Account

	DR	CR
Net Wages	6,779.16	
PAYE	384.35	
Employee's NI	241.24	
Employer's NI	280.78	
	7,685.53	

The £6,779.16. is the Net Wages paid, transferred from the Net Wages Account.

The £384.35 is the total PAYE Tax deducted from employee's wages for the year.

The £241.24 is the total employees' NI deducted for the year.

The £280.78 is the total **employer's NI contribution** computed for the year.

The PAYE & NI figures are extracted from a wages summary, which is filed in **section M** on the Accounts file.

Adding the four figures gives a total of £7,685.53. This is the total wages cost to the business and its what we record on the profit and Loss Account.

PAYE /NIC CONTROL ACCOUNT

Taxes and national insurance contributions are deducted on behalf of Inland Revenue, the tax authority.

An account is prepared to show what was collected, the amount already paid to Inland Revenue, and any amounts not yet paid over.

What we prepare is the PAYE /NIC control account. On the following page is an illustration.

New Fashions

April 2006 to March 2007

PAYE /NIC Control Account

	DR	CR
Balance as at 1st april 2006		82.50
PAYE		384.35
Employee NI		241.24
Employers NI		280.78
Paid by Bank	913.34	
Balance as at 31st March 2007	75.53	
	988.87	**988.87**

There is an **opening balance** of **£82.50.** This is the amount owed to Inland Revenue at the beginning of the year. Its extracted from the previous year's balance sheet among current liabilities.

The **£384.35** is the total **PAYE tax** deducted.

The **£241.24** is the total **employees' NIC** deducted.

The **£280.78** is the total employer's NI contribution.

The **£913.34** is the **total paid** to Inland Revenue during the year.

The **£75.53** is the **amount due** to Inland Revenue, that is not yet paid by the year end. This is recorded among current liabilities on the balance sheet.

The PAYE and NI figures in the credit column are the same as the ones on the Gross wages account in the debit column.

THE WAGES CONTROL ACCOUNT

The wages control account is prepared, to confirm if the records on the net wages account, the gross wages account, and PAYE /NIC control account are correct.

It also shows if the net amount paid to employees is correct. To satisfy these functions, this control account should have a zero balance, or the totals should be the same, as illustrated below;

New Fashions

April 2006 to March 2007

Wages Control Account

	DR	CR
Net wages	6,779.16	
PAYE	384.35	
Employee's NI	241.24	
Employer's NI	280.78	
Total wages cost		7,685.53
	7,685.53	**7,685.53**
	-	

All the figures on the debit side are extracted from the wages summary filed in section N.

Adding them up gives £7,685.58, This is recorded on the right hand and this account is left with a zero balance.

This leaves us satisfied that what is recorded does not have errors.

If the total on the gross wages account is different from what we have on the control account, it shows there is an error somewhere. This has to be investigated and corrected before continuing.

TAXES

In addition to PAYE and National Insurance on wages and salaries, tax is paid on profits made in a business. If there is no profit, then there is no tax to pay.

Businesses which operate as Sole Traders or Partnerships do not pay taxes directly. The profit is treated as an income to the owners. Its the owners who are taxed on their income, and this includes the profits made in their business.

However, the profit on the profit and loss account is adjusted for tax purposes.

Those expenses which are not allowed for tax purposes are added back, and special allowances deducted instead.

For example, depreciation is added back. A special type of depreciation called **capital allowances** is instead deducted. The difference is that these are computed following special guidelines taken from the Inland Revenue Department.

When computing personal tax, personal allowances are deducted and this reduces the amount to pay.

The tax due amount, is passed on to clients who are then responsible for paying tax.

Its limited companies which pay taxes directly on their profits, since they are an independent entity. What they pay is called **corporation tax**.

THE VAT CONTROL ACCOUNT

VAT is Value Added Tax. It's a tax paid when an expenditure is made.

Small businesses whose total sales are below **£64,000,** are not required to register for VAT.

This means they do not charge or add VAT to their selling price. They do not deduct VAT from their expenses. And they do not prepare VAT quarterly reports for the Customs & Excise Tax Department.

We used a small business not registered for VAT, in our scenario and that is why there is previously no mention of VAT.

If a business is registered for VAT, it has to collect VAT tax for the Government. It does this by adding a percentage to its selling price. There are several VAT rates, but the standard one is 17.5%.

When a registered business pays VAT as part of its expenses, its supposed to claim it back. So the actual expense is net, or less by the amount of VAT paid.

The VAT collected is submitted to the Customs & Excise Tax Department on a quarterly basis. This is accompanied by a report known as a **VAT Return.**

On this report we show; the total VAT collected **(Output VAT)**, the total VAT paid on expenses **(Input VAT),** and the difference.

If the VAT collected is **more** than the VAT paid, the difference is paid to the Customs & Excise Department.

If the VAT collected is **less** than the VAT paid, the difference is claimed from the Customs & Excise Department. It comes as a **VAT refund.**

VAT Returns are prepared for every 3 months. At the end of the year, a summary is prepared. To show the total input and output VAT.

This is finalized with a VAT control account as illustrated on the following page.

VAT Control Account	DR	CR
Balance as at 1st April 2006		785.93
Output VAT		7507.99
Input VAT	3,645.81	
Paid to HMCE	4,058.38	
Balance as at 31st March 2007	589.73	
	8,293.92	8,293.92
	-	

The balance on the first of April is what was owed to the VAT Department at the beginning of year.

The output VAT of £7,507.99 is the total collected for the year.

The input VAT of £3,645.81 is the total paid by the business for the year.

The total due to the VAT department is computed by deducting the input VAT

from the output VAT. The amount is **£3,862.18.**

However, the opening balance of £785.93 increases the amount due to **£4,648.11.**

When we deduct the total amount paid in the year- **£4,058.38,** this leaves a balance of **£589.73.** This is what the business owes to the VAT Department by the year end. This is recorded on the balance sheet as a current liability.

The total VAT paid is extracted from the VAT column in the payments analysis.

The working papers regarding VAT are filed in **section O** in the accounts file.

Chapter 13

BUSINESS PERFORMANCE

This chapter looks at how the performance of a business is assessed.

After finalising the accounts, what is left is assessing business performance. Most clients just focus on the net profit figure. However, proper evaluation is done using analysis and interpretation methods.

Analysis is done using financial ratios. They include profitability, liquidity and management ratios.

Interpretation is the comparison of financial ratios to tell if there is an improvement or decline in performance. A comparison is also made with the Industry average.

Industry average is a ratio computed by an independent organization like the business link. It gets the average from the vast information it has on businesses in that sector.

PROFITABILITY RATIOS

Profitability Ratios asses performance by comparing profit with sales, and capital. These ratios include; the gross profit margin, net profit margin, and return on capital employed.

Gross profit margin compares gross profit to total

sales for the year. Its a measure of the margin, or the profit made on what is bought for resale. Below is the formula;

Gross Profit X 100%
Sales

From our records, the Gross profit margin is

$$\frac{24,655.41}{42,091.57} \times 100\% = \mathbf{58.57\%}$$

However, this doesn't say much on its own. It has to be compared with the gross profit margin for previous years. Its also compared with the gross profit margin for similar businesses, or the industry average.

Net profit margin compares net profit to total sales for the year. Below is the formula;

Net Profit X 100%
Sales

From our records, the net profit margin is;

$$\frac{14,003.74}{42,091.57} \times 100\% = \mathbf{33.27\%}$$

This is compared with the net profit margin for previous years, or the industry average.

Return on Capital Employed is a measure of how much profit was made for each pound or dollar invested. Below is the formula;

Net Profit X 100%
Capital Employed

LIQUIDITY RATIOS

Liquidity Ratios measure the ability of a business to pay off its current liabilities, or debts due within 12 months. The most used are the current ratio and quick assets ratio.

The current ratio measures the ability to pay off debts due within one year (Current liabilities), using cash or current assets that will be turned into cash within the next 12 months. Below is the formula;

Current Assets
Current Liabilities

The current ratio from our records is;

$$\frac{8,744.64}{1,250.00} = 6.99$$

If the ratio is less than one, there is cause for concern. However, the one for this business is much higher than 1, its because it doesn't buy on credit.

A Quick Assets Ratio is where stock is eliminated from the current assets, since it may take long to sell or convert into cash.

It measures the ability to pay off Current liabilities using quick assets. **Quick assets** refers to cash, and the other current assets which can be converted into cash within 8 weeks.

Below is a formula for the quick assets ratio;

Current Assets - Stock
Current Liabilities

The quick ratio from our records is;

$$\frac{(8,744.64 - 1420)}{1,250.00} = 5.86$$

The quick ratio is much higher than 1 since the business doesn't buy on credit.

EFFICIENCY RATIOS

Efficiency Ratios include stock holding days, debtor days, and creditor days.

Stock holding days measure how long it took to sell items in stock. Below is the formula;

$$\frac{\text{Average Stock}}{\text{Cost of Sales}} \times 365 \text{ days}$$

The average stock is valued at cost price. Its the average of opening and closing stock.

From our records the stock holding days were **26.89**

Debtor Days measure the average number of days taken by a debtor to pay.

A Debtor is a customer sold to on credit and they pay later. Below is the formula for debtor days;

$$\frac{\text{Debtors}}{\text{Credit Sales}} \times 365 \text{ days}$$

Debtor days can't be computed from our records since there are no debtors.

A high figure indicates that debtors are being allowed excessive debt.

Creditor Days measure the average number of days it took to pay a creditor. **A Creditor** is a business bought from on credit.

This ratio shows if a business is taking full advantage of credit available to it. Below is the formula for creditor days;

$$\frac{\text{Creditors}}{\text{Credit Purchases}} \times 365 \text{ days}$$

Creditor days can not be computed since there are no creditors in the business scenario used.

Chapter 14

CREDIT AND THE LEDGER

This chapter briefly looks at credit transactions and the ledger.

A credit transaction is where full payment is made after receiving the goods or service. The buyer is allowed to pay after 30 to 90 days.

All the previous chapters have looked at cash transactions, where full payment is made before receiving the goods or service.

However, if its a bill where a buyer is required to pay soon after receiving an invoice, it may not be classified as a credit transaction.

A business may buy on credit and sell for cash only. Suppliers bought from on credit, are **creditors**. In this case the business has creditors only, no debtors.

Some businesses buy and sell on credit. The buyers on credit are known as **debtors**. In this case the business has both debtors and creditors.

Businesses buying or selling on credit need the ledger for recording accounts. They are used to monitor the amounts owed by each individual buyer, or amounts owed to each individual supplier.

THE LEDGER

The ledger is a book where accounts are recorded. Its a specially designed book where the required lines and columns are printed in advance. Below is an illustration of the columns we find in a ledger book;

Debit side						Credit side	
Date	Details	Folio	Amount	Date	Details	Folio	Amount

A ledger book has these columns printed on all its pages. It has a **debit side** on the left hand side, and a **credit side** on the right hand side. There is a double line in the middle to separate the two. Each of the sides has columns for the date, details, folio, and amount.

In the details column is written a word or two about the transaction recorded. In the folio column is written the page or account number where the corresponding entry is recorded using the double entry method.

An account is a record of transactions between the business and a particular item, a buyer, or a seller. An account is recorded for each asset, expense or payment, income or receipt, and all others.

An account is created by demarcating a particular page in the ledger, for recording transactions about a particular item, debtor or creditor.

When a page is demarcated, we write the title of the account, or what it has been reserved for. Below is an illustration;

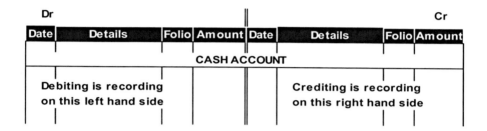

The **Dr** is an abbreviation for the debit side, while the **Cr** is an abbreviation for the credit side.

The columns on an account are the ones already printed in the ledger book. Remember the ledger book is printed for recording accounts.

Recording on ledger accounts follows the **double entry principle**. This is where every transaction is recorded twice, once on the receiving account, and once on the giving account.

What is received and given are **values expressed in money terms.** Before any account receives, another account must give.

On the account receiving, the transaction is recorded

on the **debit side**. On the account giving, the transaction is recorded on the **credit side**.

For **assets, expenses, and drawings**, their accounts are debited when a payment is made. This means the transaction is recorded on the left hand side of their accounts.

For the account where payment is coming from, its **credited**. This means the transaction is recorded on the right hand side of their account.

For an **income** like sales, its account is credited when a sale is made. When the business receives payment from a sale, the cash or bank account is debited since its the one receiving.

For a **liability** like a bank loan, its account is credited. Its treated like it's the one giving away money. If the loan is transferred to the account in the bank, the bank account in the ledger book is debited.

If the owners bring in money, the cash or bank account is debited while the Capital account is credited.

On the following page is an illustration of what the cash account looks like, if its not recorded in the receipts and payments analysis.

If the account was balanced on the 7th of April, the cash available is £127.13, as illustrated on the following page.

Dr   **Cr**

Date	Details	Folio	Amount	Date	Details	Folio	Amount
			CASH ACCOUNT				
1-Apr-06	Balance b/d		124.00	4-Apr-06	Drawings		140.00
1-Apr-06	Takings		137.85	7-Apr-06	Banking		650.00
3-Apr-06	Takings		64.85				
4-Apr-06	Takings		150.35				
5-Apr-06	Takings		153.00				
6-Apr-06	Takings		187.67				
7-Apr-06	Takings		99.65		Balance c/d		127.37
			917.37				917.37
	Balance b/d		127.37				

Ledger accounts have not been used in our basic model, in this book. The reasons are, they are the long way round, and they require more time to understand the concept of double entry.

The ledger account looked at so far is the conventional **'T' account**. In addition to having the debit and credit sides, its said to be **horizontal**. Next we look at vertical accounts.

VERTICAL ACCOUNTS

A vertical account is one where the debit and credit amount columns are laid vertically next to each, and there is an extra column for the balance. The date, details, and folio columns are catered for.

On the following page is an illustration using the same information on the cash account above.

Date	Details	Folio	Value In Debit	Value Out Credit	Balance
			CASH ACCOUNT		
1-Apr-06	Balance b/d				124
1-Apr-06	Takings		137.85		261.85
3-Apr-06	Takings		64.85		326.70
4-Apr-06	Takings		150.35		477.05
4-Apr-06	Drawings			140	337.05
5-Apr-06	Takings		153.00		490.05
6-Apr-06	Takings		187.67		677.72
7-Apr-06	Takings		99.65		777.37
7-Apr-06	Banking			650	**127.37**
			793.37	790.00	**127.37**

Instead of the debit side we have a debit column. Instead of the credit side we have a credit column. The date, details, and folio columns are shared. We simplify by referring to the debit column as the **value in column**. We refer to the credit column as the **value out column.**

We are able to calculate the balance after entries on each row. For example, with an opening balance of £124, after recording takings on the 4th of April, the balance rises to £261.85. When a figure is recorded in the value out column like the drawings of £140 on the 4th of April, the balance falls.

Its easier to calculate the balance on this account on every row, than the conventional 'T' account. So this kind of account is also known as **"The Running Balance Account".**

If there is no need to calculate the balance on each row, its done once at the end of the period. You simply get the separate totals for the debit and credit columns.

You add the debit total-£793.37, to the opening balance-£124, and deduct the credit total-£790. The answer you get is **£127.37**, which is the same as the one generated from the running balance method.

The vertical layout is more modern, user friendly, and its the one used in computerised accounting software

LEDGER SECTIONS

If transactions are not recorded in analysis books but the ledger, then we use its 3 major sections as illustrated below;

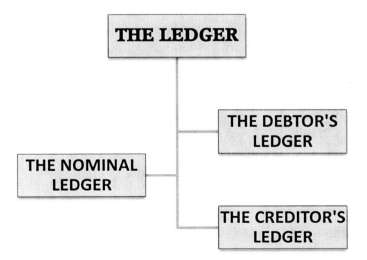

The Nominal ledger

This is the main section of the ledger, where all accounts not involving debtors and creditors are recorded. This includes the cash and bank accounts, income and expense accounts, the drawings, capital, stock and liability accounts.

If a business does not buy or sell on credit, all its transactions are recorded in this nominal ledger.

The Debtor's Ledger

In this ledger section is where we record accounts for debtors only. **Debtors** are customers allowed to buy on credit and pay later.

An account is opened for each debtor, to monitor how much they owe. There is more on debtors in the following chapter.

The Creditor's Ledger

In this ledger section is where we record accounts for creditors only. **Creditors** are suppliers who accept to sell to the business on credit.

An account is opened for each creditor, to monitor how much is owed to them. There is more on creditors in the following chapters.

For all the previous chapters in this book, ledger was not used. The reason is, we focused on a cash business where accounts are not regularly required.

They were only used for the monthly, quarterly, or yearly control accounts.

Chapter 15

DEBTORS

This chapter briefly looks at the recording of debtor's transactions.

Debtors are those who buy and pay later after 30 to 90 days.

If a customer is allowed to buy on credit, an account is opened for them. All they buy, return, and payments from them are recorded on that account.

This is done to monitor what is owed by each debtor.

Below is a debtor's vertical account illustrated;

Angela's Account

Date	Details	Fol	Value In Debit	Value Out Credit	Balance
03-Apr	Sales		460		460
13-Apr	Sales		330		790
30-Apr	Banking			450	340

In the **'value in' column** we record what is sold to them. Information is copied from the written invoice.

The corresponding entry for this is made on the sales account if we use the nominal ledger.

In case of the receipts analysis, we record this in the **'credit sales' column.** The column allocated to this is among the receipts classification, just next to banking. This is illustrated below;

New Fashions
Receipts Analysis
April 2006

		Receipt Methods					Receipts Classification			
						Credit				
Date	Cash	Banking	On Credit	Takings	Sales	Debtors	Deposits	Interest	Loans
1-Apr-06	137.85	3,000.00		137.85					3,000.00
3-Apr-06	64.85	-		64.85					
3-Apr-06			460.00		460.00				
4-Apr-06	150.35	-		150.35					
5-Apr-06	153.00	-		153.00					
6-Apr-06	187.67	-		187.67					
7-Apr-06	99.65	650.00		99.65			650.00		
8-Apr-06	168.40	-		168.40					
10-Apr-06	86.25	-		86.25					
11-Apr-06	174.25	-		174.25					
12-Apr-06	129.75	-		129.75					
13-Apr-06	158.45	-		158.45					
13-Apr-06			330.00		330.00				
14-Apr-06	158.50	-		158.50					
15-Apr-06	60.50	-		60.50					
17-Apr-06	91.00	-		91.00					
18-Apr-06	118.00	-		118.00					
19-Apr-06	145.50	-		145.50					
20-Apr-06	112.48	-		112.48					
21-Apr-06	147.50	950.00		147.50			950.00		
22-Apr-06	73.65	-		73.65					
24-Apr-06	84.35	-		84.35					
25-Apr-06	124.00	-		124.00					
26-Apr-06	154.75	-		154.75					
27-Apr-06	137.82	-		137.82					
28-Apr-06	124.45	-		124.45					
29-Apr-06	114.20	11.07		114.20				11.07	
30-Apr-07		450.00					450.00		
	3,157.17	5,061.07	790.00	3,157.17	790.00	450.00	1,600.00	11.07	3,000.00

Receipt Methods	9,008.24
Receipts Classification	9,008.24

The same value of credit sales is recorded in **"On Credit"** column. Remember every figure in the analysis is recorded **twice**. The aim is to ensure that what is recorded, and the additions are correct. This is the function which replaces the need for a trial balance.

When the debtor pays the £450 on the 30th of April, the amount is recorded in their credit or value out column. This reduces what they owe. If you look at the debtor's account on page 99, the amount owed falls from £790 to £340.

The corresponding entry for this on the receipts analysis is made in the Debtor's column among the receipts classification. This is illustrated on the previous page.

The second entry in the receipts analysis is made in the banking column. The debtor paid by direct debit, directly to the bank account.

Accounts for debtors are recorded in a separate section known as the **debtor's ledger.**

A debtor's control account is prepared at the year end. This is to ensure that all information regarding debtors was recorded properly, and that there are no errors.

Individual debtor balances are the amounts still owed by each debtor at the year end.

The balance on the control account is compared with the total of individual debtor balances. There should be no difference in the figures, and that is how we confirm there are no errors.

So the debtor's balance is recorded among **current assets** on the **balance sheet**.

However, if the debtor's total and the control account balance are different, it means there is an error. This is investigated and corrected before continuing with the accounts preparation at the year end.

Bad Debts

Bad debts is that money which is not expected to be recovered from debtors.

When the debt recovery procedures have been exhausted without success, the debt is written off to the profit and loss account. Its treated as an expense to the business. It reduces the net profit, or increases the net loss.

This problem is only experienced by businesses which sell on credit.

Chapter 16

CREDITORS

This chapter briefly looks at the recording of creditor's transactions.

Creditors are suppliers not paid immediately but after 30 to 90 days.

A separate ledger is kept for them known as the **creditor's ledger.** Its used for creditor's accounts only.

Each creditor's transactions are recorded on the account allocated to them. Below is an illustration;

Bee Wear Account			Value In	Value Out	
Date	Details	Fol	Debit	Credit	Balance
05-Apr	Purchases			515	515
09-Apr	Bank		500		15
16-Apr	Purchases			340	355

When the business buys on credit from them, the amount is recorded in their credit or **value out** column. An example is the £515 on the 5th of April.

If the nominal ledger is used, the corresponding entry would be on the purchases account.

However, in the case of the **payments analysis**, the corresponding entry is made in the **purchases column**.

The second entry is made in the **"On Credit"** column. This is allocated a column among the **payment methods,** just next to bank or credit card.

When the creditor is paid by cheque, the amount is recorded in their debit or **value in** column since they receive the money.

If the nominal ledger is used, the corresponding entry is made on the bank account.

However, in the case of the **payments analysis**, the corresponding entry is made in the creditor's column. They are allocated a column among the payment analysis next to fixed assets.

The second entry is made in the bank column if it was paid by cheque. We use the respective **payment method column**.

A **creditor's control account** is prepared at the year end.

This is to ensure that all information regarding creditors was recorded properly, and there are no errors.

Individual creditor balances are the amounts still owed by each creditor at the year end.

The balance on the control account is compared with the total of individual creditor balances. There should be no difference in the figures, and that is how we confirm there are no errors.

So the creditor's balance is recorded among **current liabilities** on the **balance sheet**.

However, if the creditor's total and the control account balance are different, it means there is an error. This is investigated and corrected before continuing with the accounts preparation at the year end.

Chapter 17

THE TRIAL BALANCE AND SUSPENSE ACCOUNT

This chapter briefly looks at the Trial balance and Suspense account.

A Trial balance is a statement compiled to ensure double entry and the balancing of accounts was done properly in the ledger. Below is an illustration;

New Fashions

Trial Balance ast as at 31st March 2007

	Debit	Credit
Sales		42,091.57
Interest		126.87
Capital		1,839.00
Loan		1,500.00
Motor vehicles	3,000.00	
Furniture	425.00	
Drawings	7,385.60	
Purchases	17,706.16	
Direct Expenses	54.50	
Salaries & Wages	4,159.92	
Premises Costs	3,120.00	
Repairs &	29.50	
Gen Admin	271.30	
Motor Expenses	236.80	
Legal & Professional	150.00	
charges	226.96	
Interest Charges	179.12	
Sundry Expenses	137.95	
Cash	449.71	
Bank	6,874.93	
Stock	1,150.00	
	45,557.44	45,557.44

This trial balance is prepared after all transactions have been recorded on ledger accounts, following the double entry principle.

At the end of the period, all accounts are balanced. Balancing is finding out the difference between the figures debited and those credited on a particular account.

A total for each of the debit and credit sides is got. We calculate the difference between the totals, and its recorded on the side with a smaller total.

If the balance is recorded on the debit side then its a **debit balance**. If its recorded on the credit side then its a **credit balance**.

Its the balance on each account that we record on the trial balance. Debit balances are recorded in the **debit column** on the trial balance. Credit balances are recorded in the **credit column** on the trial balance.

In the debit column we record balances from accounts for current and fixed assets, drawings, all expense accounts, opening stock, and debtors.

In the credit column we record balances from accounts for sales, other income, capital, loans, creditors, and other liabilities.

Independent totals for all figures in the debit and credit columns are got. The two totals should be the same if there is no error in the double entry recording and balancing of accounts.

If there is an error, the two totals on the trial balance **are not the same**. That is how the trial balance exposes errors.

Since the ledger is not comprehensively used in our scenario, we didn't prepare a trial balance. It was not required.

However, if you closely check the balances on the previous page, they are the same as the totals generated on the receipts and payments analyses in chapter 7. The exceptions we have are for the cash, bank, and loan balances which we generated on their control accounts.

If all transactions are recorded in the ledger following double entry principle, bookkeeping ends with the trial balance.

That is when the recording is confirmed to be correct and the accounting phase takes over.

With the exception of adjustments, figures used on the profit and loss account, and balance sheet come from the trial balance.

THE SUSPENSE ACCOUNT

This is an account where we temporarily record transactions we are not sure about. For example, when recording an invoice from an unfamiliar supplier, and what they supplied is not clear.

Instead of guessing and recording it on the wrong account, its temporarily recorded on the suspense account. When the client clarifies what exactly it was, the amount is transferred to the correct account.

The suspense account is also **used when the trial balance has exposed errors.** When the errors are corrected, there is no balance left on the suspense account, and that's the end of it. It does not appear on the final accounts.

If the bookkeeping is done using analysis books, the amount we are unsure about is temporarily recorded in a suspense column.

When clarification is got, the amount is transferred to the correct column. Transferring is quite easy when recording on a spreadsheet.

Chapter 18

ACCOUNTING PRINCIPLES AND CONCEPTS

This chapter briefly explains the rules and regulations guiding the bookkeeping and Accounts preparation.

Bookkeeping and Accounting is done following a set of rules and regulations known as **Accounting Principles and Concepts.**

They have been developed by authorities in the Accounting and Tax professions, over a long period of time. Their aim is to have uniformity in the recording of transactions, and the preparation of Accounts.

They include; the consistency concept; the business entity concept; the historical cost concept, the going concern concept, the matching concept, the prudence concept, the money measurement concept, the materiality concept, the time interval concept, the realisation concept, and the duality concept.

However, some concepts are more important than others. When there is a conflict, one concept is followed and the other is ignored. Below is a brief explanation for each.

The Consistency Concept

This concept requires Bookkeepers and Accountants to stick to the chosen method of preparing accounts, from one year to another.

This is because there is more than one accepted method of preparing certain figures and statements.

Consistency is important when comparing performance for different years, and among different businesses.

The Business Entity Concept

This concept stresses the need to separate personal issues from the business. As much as possible, personal issues are not entered in the business' records.

If business funds are used for personal payments, they are recorded in the drawings column or account.

The Historical Cost Concept

According to this concept, fixed assets are recorded at their original purchase price, and not current market value.

The current market value may be an inaccurate estimate, yet the historical value can be backed up by invoices or receipts.

Although we consider the net book value of fixed assets on the balance sheet, we do include notes to the accounts. They show the historical cost and depreciation. The detailed working is filed in section E, on the accounts file.

The Going Concern Concept

According to this concept, the value of fixed assets recorded on a balance sheet depends on whether the business is closing down, or its continuing to operate.

If its continuing to operate, fixed assets are recorded at the net book value. However, if its closing down in the next few months, the assets are recorded at the amount they can be sold for.

The Matching Concept

According to this concept, expenses should be matched with incomes for the same financial year, on the profit and loss account.

Although opening stock is bought the previous year, the year in which its sold is when its recorded on the profit and loss account. That is when it becomes a part of the cost of sales, or an expense.

So the expense on that stock in the previous year, was not written off to the profit and loss account. While its still stock in the business, it's a current asset on the balance sheet.

This is the reason why we deduct the cost of sales and not purchases, from sales to get gross profit.

The Prudence Concept

According to this concept, a gain or profit should not be recorded unless there is certainty. On the other hand, anticipated losses should be provided for immediately.

This is the reason why there is a provision for doubtful debts. Debts whose recovery is doubted, are provided for on the profit and loss account. This is done even if they are not yet written off as bad debts.

The Realization Concept

This concept is to do with, the right moment when a credit transaction is recognized as a sale.

Is it recognized when the goods pass on to the buyer; when the invoice is sent to the buyer; or when payment is received.

There needs to be uniformity about which procedure to apply. A cash sale is recognized immediately since payment is received on the spot.

The Time Interval Concept

According to this concept, accounts should be prepared at regular intervals of one year, or 12 months. Each business decides the starting month for its financial year. The 12th month becomes automatic.

The Materiality Concept

According to this concept, transactions of high value should be treated separately. Those with low value can be grouped together or ignored.

Its transactions of high value which are said to be **material**. They are the ones which have a reasonable impact on the accounts and our judgment.

If a transaction is immaterial, its absence or grouping with others will not have an effect on our judgment.

However, what is material to a small business, may be

immaterial to a big business which has a high sales turnover.

The Money Measurement Concept

This concept restricts Bookkeeping and accounting to only those issues which have a financial value. If they don't have a money value then they can't be recorded.

The Duality Concept

The word dual means two. According to this concept, each and every transaction must have **two effects** in the ledger, which are equal and opposite to each other.

For every debit entry, there is a credit entry that is equal and opposite to it.

This concept is the basis of the **double entry principle** used when recording transactions in the ledger. Every transaction is recorded twice, once on the debit side and once on the credit side of another account.

Its the basis of the trial balance exposing errors, which affect double entry and the balancing in the ledger

Its also the basis of the balance sheet balancing. The net assets in the business, must be equal to the funds invested.

Chapter 19

COMPUTERISATION

Like most aspects of business these days, computers are used to prepare accounts.

We either use the spreadsheet, or proper bookkeeping and accounting software like Sage, Quick Books, Iris, and many others.

If the client is a small cash business, the spreadsheet is sufficient. However, if they have credit transactions then accounting software is used.

It speeds up the whole process. It monitors debtor and creditor account balances. It provides any required figures instantly.

All the bookkeeping and accounting illustrations in this book were prepared on a spreadsheet.

The major advantage of a spreadsheet is that you can clearly follow up what you are doing.

Using accounting software requires a proper understanding of how they operate. Otherwise you make errors and think the software is faulty. In an attempt to correct, you may worsen the situation.

So you may end up with results that don't make sense, or can't be interpreted. Remember, its **Garbage In, and Garbage Out.**

Printed in the United States
122496LV00011B/210/A